Willi ;

54 Fascinating Facts
For Kids

Paul Tyler

This book is just one of a series of "Fascinating Facts For Kids" books. For more fascinating facts about people, history, animals and more please visit:

www.fascinatingfactsforkids.com

Contents

Shakespeare's Birth

1. William Shakespeare was born over 450 years ago in the market town of Stratford-Upon-Avon in the English county of Warwickshire.

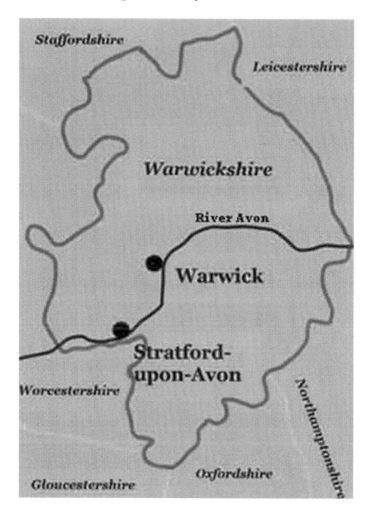

2. The exact date of Shakespeare's birth is not known, but it was probably 23 April 1564.

3. William was the eldest son of John and Mary Shakespeare. John was a successful glove maker and a respected member of the community in Stratford.

4. When William was born, a dreadful disease called the bubonic plague was sweeping through England, killing thousands of people. The disease, also called the Black Death, had originated in Asia and was brought to Europe by fleas which lived on black rats.

A black rat

5. When the Black Death reached Stratford, William was lucky to survive. The disease killed hundreds of people, including an entire family which lived on the same street as Shakespeare.

Childhood & Schooling

6. In 1568, John Shakespeare was elected as the Bailiff of Stratford, which was the most important official in the town. This meant that William could be sent, free of charge, to the town's grammar school.

7. William started his new school when he was around the age of six and was taught history, literature, poetry and Latin. No-one was allowed to speak English at the school, only Latin.

A classroom at Shakespeare's school

8. The school day was very long in Shakespeare's day. It started at six o'clock in the morning and went on until five o'clock in the afternoon. The only day off was Sunday and there were few holidays.

9. One of John Shakespeare's duties as the Bailiff of Stratford was to give permission to groups of travelling actors to put on plays in the town. William was allowed to watch these plays and he fell in love with acting and the theater.

10. It was expected that William would go to university when he had finished his schooling, but when he was around 15 years old his father fell on hard times and so William left school to help out with the glove making business.

Marriage and the 'Lost Years'

11.   When he was 18 years old, William met Anne Hathaway, a 26-year-old farmer's daughter who lived in a nearby village. They fell in love and married in November, 1582.

12.   In 1583, Anne gave birth to Susanna and two years later twins arrived - a boy called Hamnet and a girl called Judith. By the age of just 21, William was the father of three children.

13.   Little is known of the ten years of Shakespeare's life following his marriage to Anne and this decade has become known as the 'Lost Years'. But William had a family to support and needed to find paid employment.

14.   We know that William loved the theater and it is thought that he may have joined one of the companies of actors that visited Stratford. With this company he would have travelled the country learning his trade as an actor and starting to write plays.

15.   Whatever happened in the ten years following 1582, one thing is known for sure. By 1592, Shakespeare was living in London and was a successful and well-known actor and playwright.

16th Century London

16. London in the 16th century was surrounded by a city wall. Inside this wall the narrow, twisting streets were crowded and filthy. Ditches were used as toilets and the streets were full of garbage.

17. 200,000 people were crammed inside the city walls, ten times more than the population of Shakespeare's home town of Stratford.

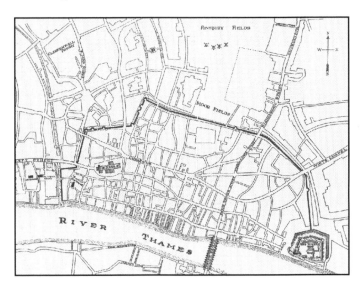

16th Century London

18. The River Thames, which separated the walled city from the south bank, was important to London. It was full of boats and ships and it provided drinking water to the city's population.

19. The only bridge over the river was London Bridge. It was more like a street than a bridge, being packed with houses, stores and chapels.

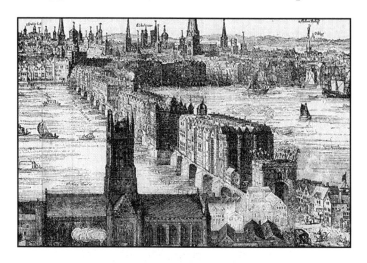

London Bridge

20. Despite its problems, London was a lively, bustling city. It was one of Europe's most important cultural centers and home to many poets, playwrights, actors and musicians. To have a career in the theater, Shakespeare had to move to London.

21. The city's authorities didn't like theaters because they attracted big crowds which often turned violent. Because of this, theaters were built outside the city walls where the authorities had no power.

Shakespeare in London

22. Shakespeare lived in London alone, having left his family back home in Stratford. As London was so dirty and crowded, perhaps William decided it was not the ideal place to raise children.

23. Shakespeare saw his wife and three children once a year when he made the 100-mile journey from London to Stratford, which took two days on horseback.

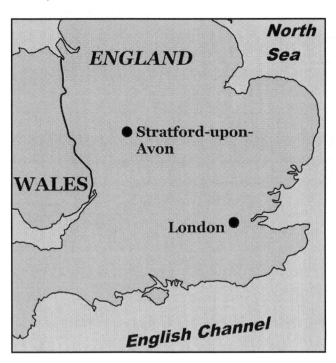

24. In London, Shakespeare joined a theater group called 'The Lord Chamberlain's Men', who rented a playhouse called 'The Theatre'. William worked for the group as an actor and also wrote plays for them to perform.

25. The Lord Chamberlain's Men became the leading theater company in London and often performed at the court of Queen Elizabeth I.

Queen Elizabeth I

26. In 1592, the Black Death broke out in London again. All the theaters were closed down so that the disease wouldn't spread through the audiences.

27. As no theater performances were possible during the time of the Black Death, Shakespeare concentrated on writing poetry. One poem, 'The Rape of Lucrece', was written for the Earl of Southampton, who is said to have paid William £1,000 for it.

The Earl of Southampton

28. Shakespeare wrote 154 sonnets - which are 14-line poems - between 1592 and 1598. They were published in 1609 and became some of Shakespeare's most popular works.

29. By 1594, London was at last free from the plague and the theaters opened again. Shakespeare now concentrated on writing plays.

The Plays

30. Unusually for the time, Shakespeare was employed as the resident playwright for the Lord Chamberlain's Men, meaning that this was the only company that got to perform Shakespeare's plays.

31. William had to produce new plays regularly and he worked very hard, writing two or three plays a year as well as acting with the Lord Chamberlain's Men. He was to write 37 plays during the course of his life.

32. Not all Shakespeare's plays are completely original. The pressure he was under to produce new plays on a regular basis meant that he sometimes borrowed plots and characters from old stories. This was common practice at the time as other playwrights did the same thing.

33. Shakespeare was an extremely versatile playwright, writing plays on many different subjects. He wrote historical plays, comedies and tragedies.

34. Some of Shakespeare's earliest plays are the 'Histories', based on the lives of English kings, such as Richard II, Richard III, Henry IV and Henry V. He often altered the historical facts to make his plays more exciting.

35. Shakespeare's comedies include 'Much Ado About Nothing', 'A Midsummer Night's Dream' and 'Twelfth Night'. His comedies were often love stories with lots of silliness and misunderstandings, but having a happy ending.

A scene from Twelfth Night

36. Many people think that Shakespeare's tragedies are his finest works. They include 'Julius Caesar', 'Hamlet' and 'Othello'. They are often blood-curdling stories that end with the death of the leading character.

Wealth, Fame & a New Theater

37. Shakespeare's plays brought him fame and wealth. By 1597 he had made enough money to buy the second-largest house in Stratford, where he was to spend more time with his family.

38. Over the years, Shakespeare was to buy more and more land in Stratford which provided income from rent, meaning that he and his family would have enough money for the rest of their lives.

39. In 1598, the theater where the Lord Chamberlain's Men performed was closed down and Shakespeare and his fellow actors had to find a new home.

40. It was decided to build a new theater on the south side of the River Thames. It was called the 'Globe' and it opened in the summer of 1599.

The site of the Globe

41. The Globe was one of the finest theaters in London, holding an audience of 2,500 people. The actors in the company shared the money that was made from the performances.

42. In 1603, Queen Elizabeth died and King James I was crowned king. The new king loved the theater and gave support to Shakespeare and his fellow actors. The company changed its name to 'The King's Men' and often performed at the court of King James.

43. Shakespeare continued to write wonderful new plays for the next decade until 1613. It was in this year that during a performance of 'Henry VIII', a spark from a faulty cannon set the roof of the Globe on fire. Within an hour the theater had burnt to the ground.

44. Luckily, nobody was hurt during the fire, although one member of the audience had to have his burning breeches put out with a bottle of beer.

The Last Years

45.   Following the fire at the Globe, Shakespeare decided to retire from the theater and return to Stratford. He was 49 years old and wanted to spend his later years with his family.

46.   By 1616, Shakespeare's health had got worse and he decided to make will. He left most of his property, money and land to members of his family and also left money to the poor people of Stratford.

47.   Shakespeare had written his will just in time, as on 23 April 1616, exactly 52 years after he was born, he died at his home. He was buried two days later at Holy Trinity Church, Stratford.

48.   After his death, two members of the King's Men arranged for the publication of Shakespeare's plays. They appeared in 1623, ensuring that future generations would be able to enjoy some of the greatest dramas ever written.

Assorted Shakespeare Facts

49.   Shakespeare has become known as the 'Bard of Avon'. Bard means 'great poet' and the Avon is the river that runs through Shakespeare's home town of Stratford.

50.   Shakespeare invented thousands of words and phrases, with many becoming part of everyday English. Examples include: 'All that glitters is not gold', 'break the ice', 'cold-blooded' and 'bedroom'.

51.   Although Shakespeare had three children, his only son, Hamnet, died in 1596 at the age of just eleven.

52.   Anne Hathaway died in 1623 and was buried beside her husband at Holy Trinity Church in Stratford.

53.   In 1670, Shakespeare's grand-daughter, Elizabeth, died. She was his last surviving grand-child and with her death Shakespeare's family line came to an end.

54.   The Globe Theatre was rebuilt in 1997 very close to the original site, thanks to American actor and director Sam Wanamaker. Visitors from all over the world come to watch Shakespeare's plays there.

The new Globe Theater

Conclusion

William Shakespeare rose from relatively humble beginnings in a small market town in the English Midlands to become the greatest playwright the country has ever seen.

His plays are as popular today as they have ever been and are still relevant to the modern world, dealing with all types of human behavior and situations that we can all recognize.

For more than 400 years Shakespeare has been a huge influence on other playwrights, painters, musicians and poets, and this will surely continue for many years to come.

As a fellow playwright of the time, Ben Jonson, wrote in tribute to Shakespeare following his death:

'He was not of an age, but for all time'

For more in the Fascinating Facts For Kids series, please visit:

www.fascinatingfactsforkids.com

Illustration Attributions

Cover Image   {{PD-1923}}

Title Page Image   {{PD-1923}}

A Black Rat   Welcome Images
www.wellcomeimages.org

Shakespeare's School   {{PD-1923}}

London Bridge   {{PD-1923}}

Queen Elizabeth I   {{PD-1923}}

Earl of Southampton   {{PD-1923}}

Scene from 12th Night   {{PD-1923}}